Technology Timelines

DIGITAL TECHNOLOGY

W
FRANKLIN WATTS
LONDON • SYDNEY

This edition first published in 2015
by Franklin Watts
338 Euston Road
London NW1 3BH

Franklin Watts Australia
Level 17/207 Kent Street
Sydney, NSW 2000

Copyright © 2014
Brown Bear Books Ltd

A CIP catalogue record for this book
is available from the British Library.

ISBN: 978-1-4451-3571-7

Dewey no. 004'.09

Printed in China

Franklin Watts is a division of
Hachette Children's Books,
an Hachette UK company.
www.hachette.co.uk

Note to parents and teachers concerning
websites: In the book every effort has been
made by the Publishers to ensure that
websites are suitable for children, that they
are of the highest educational value, and that
they contain no inappropriate or offensive
material. However, because of the nature of
the Internet, it is impossible to guarantee that
the contents of these sites will not be altered.
We advise that Internet access is supervised
by a responsible adult.

Author: Tom Jackson
Designer: Lynne Lennon
Picture Researcher: Clare Newman
Children's Publisher: Anne O'Daly
Design Manager: Keith Davis
Editorial Director: Lindsey Lowe

Contents

Introduction

Computers and other digital technologies are machines controlled by a set of instructions called a programme. The instructions are written as a string of digits (numbers) which a computer can understand. Today, computers are in many things from toys to telephones, but they began as machines for doing calculations.

Counting frame

An abacus is a simple calculator. It was invented at least 5,000 years ago, but it is still used in some places today. Long numbers are shown by flicking beads along columns arranged side by side. The lower section of this one counts from 1 to 5 and the upper beads show 5 and 10. Each column adds up to 15.

« A DIFFERENT VIEW »

COUNTING STONES

An ancient technique used by shepherds to count their flocks was to make a pile of pebbles – one for every sheep. The Latin word for 'pebble' is calculus, which is where we get the word 'calculate'. The stone piles were the world's first calculators!

The Pascaline

The word 'computer' was first used in 1613. It meant a person who did complicated calculations. In 1642, Frenchman Blaise Pascal invented the Pascaline, a clockwork calculator, to help these human computers. It could add up to 999,999.

Punch card loom

In 1801, the French weaver Joseph Marie Jacquard invented the first programmable machine – a loom for weaving patterned cloth. The programme was a pattern of holes punched into a set of cards. The punched cards ran through the loom telling it when to add each colour of thread to the cloth.

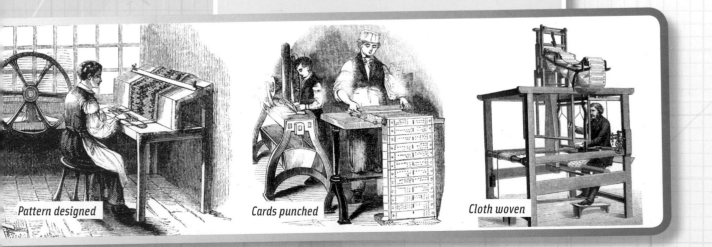

Pattern designed *Cards punched* *Cloth woven*

Difference Engine

The first computers were invented by Englishman Charles Babbage. Like today's computers, his devices followed a programme. They had a memory for storing numbers and a processor for doing calculations.

Babbage designed the Difference Engine in 1822. It was a mechanical calculator for producing tables of 'polynomial functions'. These complex numbers are used by engineers and scientists and Babbage's machine could calculate them more quickly than human 'computers'.

The Difference Engine (shown right) could only do this one thing. So, in 1837, Babbage designed the Analytical Engine. This could be programmed to perform any calculation. This second device is regarded as the first true computer. However, Babbage could not afford to build either machine.

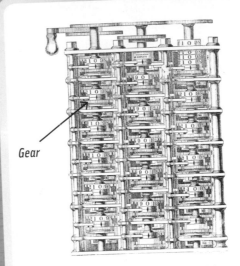

Gear

The number wheels were all fitted with a gear. The number being displayed depended on how fast each gear turned.

A HANDLE was turned to perform the calculation.

TIMELINE

1620s
Slide rule
A calculator is designed by English maths genius William Oughtred. The slide rule has a numbered ruler that moves inside another.

1865
Writing ball
The Hansen Writing Ball, invented in Denmark, is the first typewriter. The letter keys are arranged on a dome above a sheet of paper.

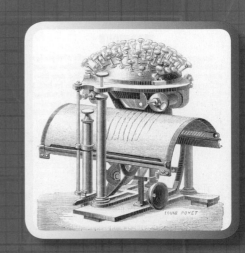

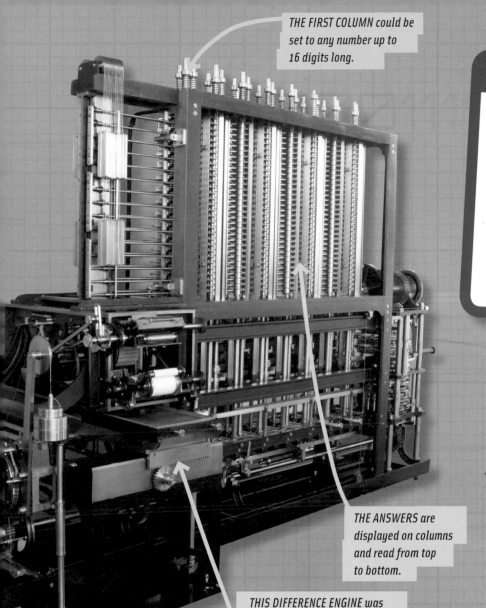

THE FIRST COLUMN could be set to any number up to 16 digits long.

ADA LOVELACE

The first programmer was Ada Lovelace. She was the daughter of the poet Lord Byron. Lovelace wrote a plan for how to programme Babbage's Analytical Engine using punched cards.

THE ANSWERS are displayed on columns and read from top to bottom.

THIS DIFFERENCE ENGINE was constructed by a museum in the 1990s. It has 25,000 parts.

1872 ▷

Tide predictor

The Scottish scientist Lord Kelvin invents a mechanical computer. It uses gears to calculate the time of tides around the world.

1890 ▷

Tabulator

The US government buys an electrical machine for handling its population data. The makers go on to start IBM, which becomes the first big computer company.

Looking at Screens

A modern computer has a screen. However, screen technology was not invented with computers in mind. The story of computer screens begins with television.

Today's televisions have evolved from a system developed by the Scottish engineer John Logie Baird in 1926. Early television screens were a glass cathode ray tube (CRT), which glowed when electrified. By 1929, Baird was sending television pictures as radio signals and in 1936 the BBC began broadcasting the world's first TV channel.

Marconiphone 707

This combined television and radio set was sold in the UK in 1938. It cost the equivalent of £2,000 in today's money. When World War II (1939–1945) began, the BBC stopped broadcasting TV until 1946.

THE SPEAKER was hidden behind a protective screen.

THE TELEVISION was tuned by turning a knob so the set picked up the strong radio signal that transmitted the pictures and sound.

TIMELINE

1906
Thermionic valve
The first electronic switches are invented. Glass valves that turn currents on and off will be used in the first electronic computers.

1910
Typewriters
The layout of the modern keyboard becomes more or less standard, using the QWERTY system.

THE SCREEN *was just 18 cm across, and the picture was black and white.*

≪ INSIDE OUT ≫

CATHODE-RAY TUBE

A cathode ray is a beam of electrons. When it hits the inside coating of a television screen, the beam makes a glowing dot. The TV signal directs a flashing beam across the screen to make a picture of tiny dots. It changes the picture about 25 times a second, which makes it look like it is moving.

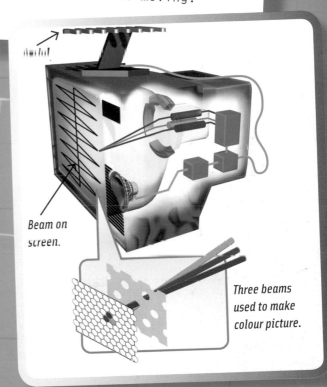

Beam on screen.

Three beams used to make colour picture.

THE WOODEN CASE *made the television fit in with other items of furniture in a 1930s house.*

1912

Harvard computers

A team of female mathematicians in America (right) work out how to measure the distance to stars using data from telescopes.

1936

The Z1

Konrad Zuse, a German inventor, begins to build the first programmable computer with a memory. The Z1 is mechanical as well as electrical.

Codebreakers

During World War II, Britain and its allies built devices for decoding secret messages sent by the enemy. The systems invented then paved the way to modern computers.

The codebreakers intercepted many coded messages. However, they did not know what they meant because the enemy used a new code every day. The codebreakers would guess at the meaning of one of the messages, and use machines to turn it back into every possible coded form. If one of the coded answers matched the actual message from the enemy, it would reveal the code system being used that day – and so all of the other messages sent that day could be decoded.

In 1939, the code-breaking machines were devices called 'Bombes'. These copied the way a German coding machine worked and did it on a huge scale.

THE LETTERS of the alphabet were written around the rotor and used to spell out messages.

THIS BOMBE is a replica built for a museum.

TIMELINE

1938
Enigma machine
The German military coding machine is upgraded to make it seemingly unbreakable. It uses letters on three wheels to jumble up a message into one of 17,500 different versions.

1940
Phone connection
American George Stibitz operates his early electronic machine, the Complex Number Calculator, using a keyboard, which is connected to it by a telephone line.

THE ROTORS were just like those used in the enemy coding machines.

ELECTRIFIED PLATES were under all the rotors.

ALAN TURING

The Englishman Alan Turing was a chief codebreaker in World War II. In 1936 he had explained how a machine could be controlled by a mathematical code. This was the start of digital technology.

WIRES at the back were used to connect rotors in a specific order.

1943

Colossus Mark 1

Codebreakers in the UK design and build the first fully electronic computer to help crack codes made by a new more complex German machine.

1946

Giant brain

The American government unveils the ENIAC (Electronic Numerical Integrator And Computer). Unlike Colossus, it is designed to perform any programme at all.

Mainframe

Computer circuits are a series of switches. Early computers used glass valves for this job, but they often broke. A new type of switch, called a transistor, made computer circuits more reliable.

Transistors were invented in America in 1947. They are made of silicon, which is a semiconductor. Semiconductors allow electricity to flow through them, but can also switch to blocking the current. A programme is simply a list of 1s and 0s. A '1' tells a switch in the circuit to turn on, while a '0' turns it off. Circuits of transistor switches were arranged on blocks of silicon, which became known as microchips.

In the 1950s and '60s governments and companies used 'mainframe' computers to store information and do difficult calculations. Unlike early valve computers a mainframe used microchips. However, it was still very big and filled a whole room.

THIS 1960S MAINFRAME was 10,000 times slower than modern personal computers.

TAPE DRIVES worked in the same way as a tape recorder, only on a much larger scale.

TIMELINE

1949
Mercury memory
A type of computer memory records data as a wave that ripples back and forth inside a tube of electrified liquid mercury.

1954
Transistors
The first silicon transistors are produced by Texas Instruments. Transistors begin to replace valves in digital technology.

MAGNETIC TAPE was used to record the results produced by the computer.

THE MONITOR screen worked in the same way as a cathode ray television set.

THE TERMINAL was where the computer was controlled from.

MICROCHIP

Instead of being connected by wires, the components on a microchip are on one piece of silicon. When it is switched on, the transistors direct electricity through the chip according to the rules set out in the programming.

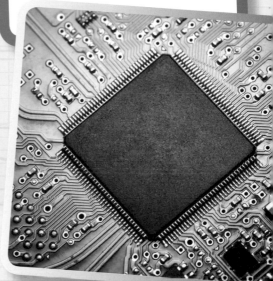

1964
Packet switching

Computer files are split into many small 'packets', each finding a different route through a network. This ensures that messages arrive, even when some connections in the network are broken.

1969
Mission control

The Apollo 11 spacecraft lands on the Moon thanks to NASA's Apollo Guidance Computer. This is one of the first computers to use microchips.

Office Tools

During the 1970s, computers began to get much smaller. New 'microcomputers' could be used for a wider range of applications.

Advances in technology meant that as computers got smaller, more businesses and people were able to use them. New 'microcomputers' did everything that a mainframe could. They were also used as 'word processors' for typing documents – and allowed users to create their own computer programmes.

THE DISK DRIVE allowed users to load files to work on and save for later use.

Osborne 1
This model from 1981 was the first portable microcomputer. It weighed 10 kg and had just 64 kilobytes of memory. That meant it could only store one document at a time!

PLUGS, OR PORTS, allowed the computer to be connected to a printer or standard telephone line.

TIMELINE

1970s
The Internet
After sending the first signal in 1969, the Internet spreads across America and connects to the UK in 1973.

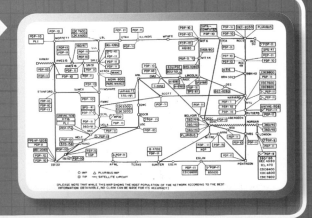

1973
Xerox Alto
A desktop computer is introduced. A forerunner of today's computers, the Alto (right) has a mouse, a keyboard and a screen that displays clickable menus.

THE TINY SCREEN measured just 12 cm diagonally from corner to corner.

FLOPPY DISKS containing useful files were stored in slots. They were much easier to carry than computer tapes.

« INSIDE OUT »

FLOPPY DISK

In the 1970s computer files were kept on flexible, or floppy, disks. The information was stored as a pattern of magnetised zones. The disks became smaller and stiffer in the 1980s.

A FOLDING LID closed up the computer so that it could be carried around.

THE KEYBOARD was laid out the same as a traditional typewriter.

1975

Microsoft

Bill Gates and Paul Allen set up a company called Microsoft to supply software for early personal computers. In less than 20 years, the success of Microsoft makes Bill Gates the world's richest person.

1977

TCP / IP

The communication protocol, or standard system, for computers linked by the Internet is agreed. The Transmission Control Protocol (TCP) and Internet Protocol (IP) have been used ever since.

Games Machines

The first computers to become common in people's homes were for playing games. Computer gaming is now a huge business. People today spend more money on games than they do on going to the cinema.

Microcomputers were difficult to use. The owners often had to programme them themselves. Games computers used the same technology but came preprogrammed. The very first, such as the Home Pong machine from 1975, came with just a single game on it. Later versions loaded a range of games from cartridges.

Atari 2600

The model of video game machine shown here was sold in 1982. It was plugged into a television aerial socket and could play dozens of games.

JUST FOUR SWITCHES were needed to control the simple computer.

A JOYSTICK was used to control 'sprites' – the moving graphics on the screen.

TIMELINE

1980s

Digital watches
Wristwatches that do not have hands but show the time as numbers on a liquid-crystal display, or LCD, screen become common (right).

1981

IBM PC
The world's largest mainframe computer company, IBM, introduces its first personal computer, known as the PC.

A GAMES CARTRIDGE was pushed into this slot before the machine was turned on.

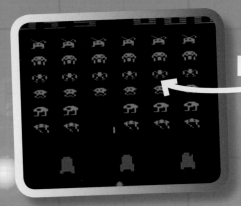

THE GRAPHICS were in colour and the games had sound effects.

VIDEO COMPUTER SYSTEM™

GAME SELECT

GAME RESET

« INSIDE OUT »

LCD SCREEN

Handheld games machines and laptops use LCD (liquid-crystal display) technology. The graphics are made from coloured dots. A dot appears when an electric current runs through a special liquid that is squashed between layers of see-through plastic.

colour LCD dots

electricity supply

THE COMPUTER PROCESSOR could only handle games designed for this machine.

1982
Arcades
Most people are playing games in shops called video arcades (left), but from now on home consoles begin to take over.

1983
Handheld games
A folding games console with two screens for playing 'Donkey Kong II' is introduced. It is the inspiration for the Nintendo DS.

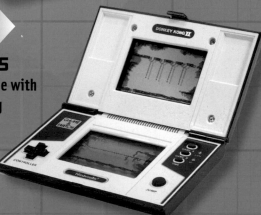

DONKEY KONG II

GAME WATCH

CONTROLLER

Nintendo

JUMP

Personal Computers

The next step in digital technology was the personal computer. These were easy to use and could be used for just about anything from writing text to drawing pictures.

The first true personal computers were introduced in the 1980s, but it took another ten years before they were cheap enough for large numbers of people to be able to buy.

User interface

The most famous early personal computer was the Apple Macintosh, which was introduced in 1984. It used a graphical user interface (GUI), where each document was shown on screen as a window and the user could control the computer by clicking on little images, or icons. By the early 1990s, all personal computers used this system.

MICROSOFT WINDOWS, the most common GUI system, became standard on PCs in 1992.

ICONS represented applications and documents. They could be clicked to open, or dragged between windows.

THE WINDOWS could be made any size. They were arranged one on top of another on the background screen, like papers on a 'desktop'.

TIMELINE

1987
Burning CDs
The first CD drives that can record files on a blank compact disc are introduced. They use a laser to 'burn' the information onto the disc.

1989
Email
The US company, Compuserve, is the first to offer an email service to the public.

1993
Browser history
The first full-scale web browser, Mosaic, is launched for looking at documents on the World Wide Web, which had been invented in 1989.

THE APPLE MACINTOSH was a single unit containing the computer and its monitor.

A DOCUMENT was shown as it would appear if printed on paper. This idea is called 'whizzy wig', or WYSIWYG – What You See Is What You Get.

hello, i am a macintosh

TIM BERNERS-LEE

In 1989, English scientist Tim Berners-Lee invented a way of sharing information on computers. Instead of sending files between machines, his idea was to let people read the files held on any machine on a network. He called it the World Wide Web.

« POWER PEOPLE »

ALL PROGRAMMES and documents were loaded from floppy disks inserted here.

THE MOUSE had a single button.

1994

Search engine

Yahoo!, standing for 'Yet Another Hierarchical Officious Oracle', is launched as a new way of finding documents on the rapidly growing Web.

1995

First wiki

A website called WikiWikiWeb allows its readers to make changes. This system becomes known as a 'wiki', which means 'quick' in Hawaiian.

A Look Inside

A personal computer is made up of many parts. The microchips and other physical components are called the hardware. The programmes that make the computer work are the software.

No computer can work without an operating system. This is the main software that makes all the other parts work together. The other software, such as the word processor or Internet browser, are known as 'applications'.

Hardware components

One of the innovations in personal computers was the hard disk (as opposed to a floppy one). A hard disk is used to store the software and other computer files. The software is run by the central processing unit (CPU) located on the 'motherboard'.

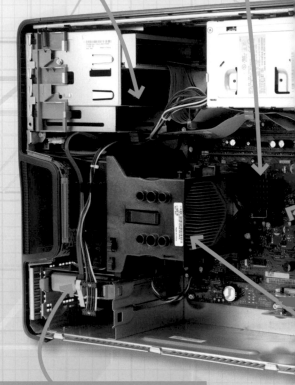

THE MOTHERBOARD is the main circuit.

DISK DRIVES read the files on CDs, DVDs and floppy disks.

THE HARD DISK is made up of magnetic plates that spin around.

TIMELINE

1996

Java
Personal computers are controlled by a range of operating systems. The Java programming language is designed so it works on all of them.

1997

CAPTCHA
Introduced to ensure that only people – not other computers – fill in forms on the Web, the CAPTCHA system asks users to read and type out a distorted word shown on the screen. Computers cannot do this.

Username: Username or e-mail
Password:
captcha (reload image)
Type the above word
Submit

THE POWER SUPPLY converts the electricity supply into a form that does not damage the sensitive components.

INKJET PRINTER

Most printers use inkjet technology. This creates text and pictures from dots of ink squirted out of cartridges. Just four inks are needed to produce any colour of the rainbow.

« INSIDE OUT »

THE RAM (random access memory) is used to store information needed to keep software running.

GRAPHICS AND VIDEOS are organised by this processor.

A FAN inside the computer blows air over the components to stop them getting too hot.

THE CPU, the main microchip, defines how fast and powerful a computer is.

1998

Google

Americans, Larry Page and Sergey Brin, set up Google, a search engine that ranks web pages in order of importance.

2001

Wikipedia

A Web-based encyclopedia, written and edited by its readers, is created by Americans Jimmy Wales and Larry Sanger. (Its logo is shown, right.)

Going Wireless

By the beginning of the 21st century, most computers were connected to the Internet. Radio technology meant you could connect to the network anywhere.

Early portable computers were very heavy, while later lightweight models could not really match the abilities of a larger 'desktop' computer. However, by 2010, mobile 'laptop' computers – so named because they sit on the lap – were just as powerful as normal desktop models.

WiFi

At first, a computer had to be plugged into the telephone system to access the Internet. Today, laptops can connect by a wireless radio signal, called WiFi. WiFi became a standard system in 1999. The signal is sent out by a router, which creates a WiFi 'hotspot'.

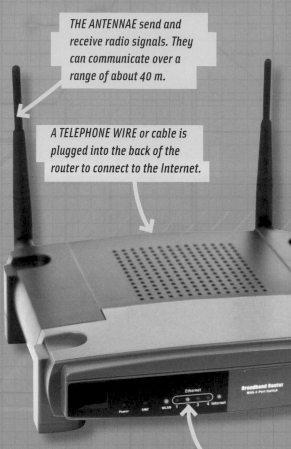

THE ANTENNAE send and receive radio signals. They can communicate over a range of about 40 m.

A TELEPHONE WIRE or cable is plugged into the back of the router to connect to the Internet.

LIGHTS on the front show if the Internet is connected and what devices are receiving signals.

TIMELINE

2004
Social network
Facebook, a website for university students to make friends, is set up by American Mark Zuckerberg. Ten years later it has 1.2 billion users.

2006
Tweeting
The Twitter Internet service is launched. Members publish short messages made up of just 140 characters or less.

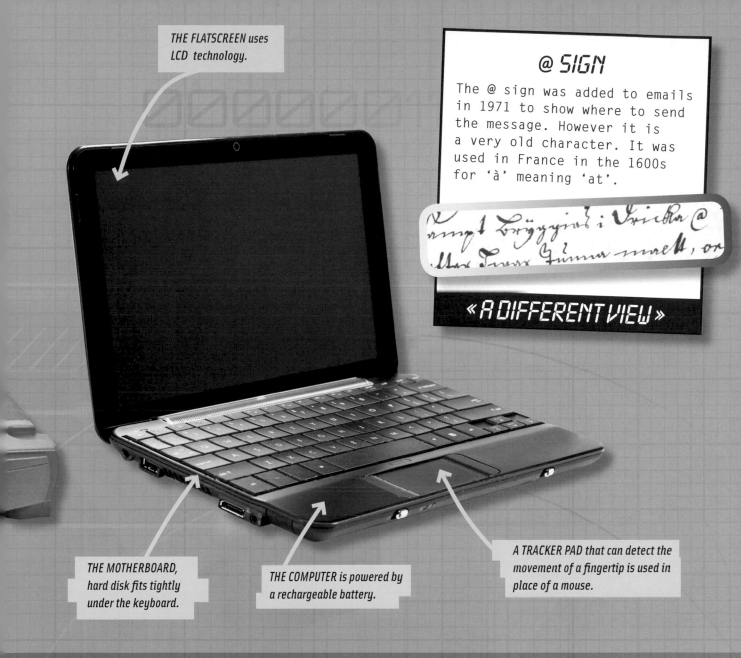

THE FLATSCREEN uses LCD technology.

@ SIGN

The @ sign was added to emails in 1971 to show where to send the message. However it is a very old character. It was used in France in the 1600s for 'à' meaning 'at'.

《 A DIFFERENT VIEW 》

THE MOTHERBOARD, hard disk fits tightly under the keyboard.

THE COMPUTER is powered by a rechargeable battery.

A TRACKER PAD that can detect the movement of a fingertip is used in place of a mouse.

2007

iPlayer
The BBC makes its radio and TV programmes available online.

2010

Tablets
Touchscreen tablet computers are launched by Apple and other major manufacturers.

In the Cloud

Cloud computing became popular in 2011. It is a system where a person's computer files – emails, pictures and documents – are not stored on their device. Instead they are accessed through the Internet when needed.

A s well as being a useful tool that can create documents and do complex calculations, a modern computer is also used to watch videos, play games and communicate with friends. There is no way all of that can fit in one computer's hard disk. Instead the files are stored in 'the cloud'. This does not mean they are up in the air, but in big data centres. One person's files will be stored in many centres all over the world. Together, these centres form a 'cloud' of computers. The cloud can be accessed via the Internet from anywhere and by a wide range of devices.

SMARTPHONES can connect to a cloud through mobile telephone networks.

TABLET COMPUTERS do not have a keyboard, but one can be displayed on the screen for use in typing.

CLOUD COMPUTING means laptops do not need large hard disks.

TIMELINE

2011
Anonymous
A worldwide hacking group (right) takes control of the computers of governments it thinks are behaving badly.

2012
Raspberry Pi
A tiny computer (right) is put on sale. It plugs into the TV and costs about a tenth of the price of other models.

APPS, OR SMALL APPLICATIONS, are on the device. The data they need to work comes from the cloud.

OPTICAL FIBRE

A file stored 'in the cloud' can be sent around the world at the speed of light along an optical fibre. The data is sent as a beam of light, which flickers to represent the 1s and 0s. The fibre's core is flexible see-through glass. The light is reflected all the way along it and could go right around the world in less than a second!

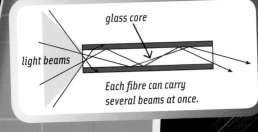

glass core

light beams

Each fibre can carry several beams at once.

THE SAME CONTENT can be accessed on different computer devices.

2013

Supercomputer

An American computer performs 10 thousand trillion calculations in a second. Months later a Chinese computer goes even faster.

Super Computers

The latest computers are designed for use in a home or in an office. They are very powerful tools used for work, communication and entertainment.

A modern computer is a work tool, television, radio, camera, telephone, music player and games machine all rolled into one. We used to need one device for each of these applications, but today's desktop computers, tablets and smartphones can do them all.

A WEBCAM films the computer user during video calls.

THE KEYBOARD AND MOUSE are not plugged into the computer. It communicates by a short-range radio connection.

VIRTUAL REALITY

Computers can create entire alternative realities, which are virtually (meaning 'almost') real. The latest games consoles use virtual reality (VR). Instead of a screen, VR is viewed through a headset. Motion sensors inside pick up any head movements, so when you turn you head the view shown moves with it. There are even VR gloves that push back on the skin when you touch objects in virtual reality.

«A DIFFERENT VIEW»

THE HIGH-DEFINITION screen can be used to show television and films streamed through the Internet.

THE SCREEN spins around and folds down over the keyboard to create a tablet-style mode.

Wind-up computer

Computers are cheaper than ever but they still need an electricity supply. This computer's battery is charged by winding a handle. Laptops like this are being used in schools in developing countries to provide the Internet in schools there.

THE COMPONENTS, such as the processor and hard disk, are located behind the screen.

THE CHARGER converts the motion of the handle into an electrical current.

THE FLATSCREEN DISPLAY is sensitive to touch.

THE MOUSE can detect several hand gestures to add extra control.

Future Computers

Digital technology has changed the world very quickly. Thirty years ago most people had never used a computer. Today they are in almost every home. What will computers be like 30 years from now?

It is hard to guess at the future of digital technology because every year brings a whole set of new uses for it. Microchip technology has advanced hugely since it was invented in the 1950s. Chips have got faster and smaller, but still work in the same basic way as the originals. There is a limit to how fast silicon-based computers can be. A new system, called quantum computing, is being investigated that – if it works – will be millions of times faster.

Computers everywhere

Instead of being a screen and keyboard on a table, computers of the future will be hidden behind the scenes. We will access them in different ways. For example, a window will also act as a touchscreen, and almost every machine we use will be online.

Brain interface

Researchers are looking at the way the brain works while we are thinking. They are trying to read thoughts from brain activity. If they succeed then we will be able to search the Internet for answers just by thinking about a question.

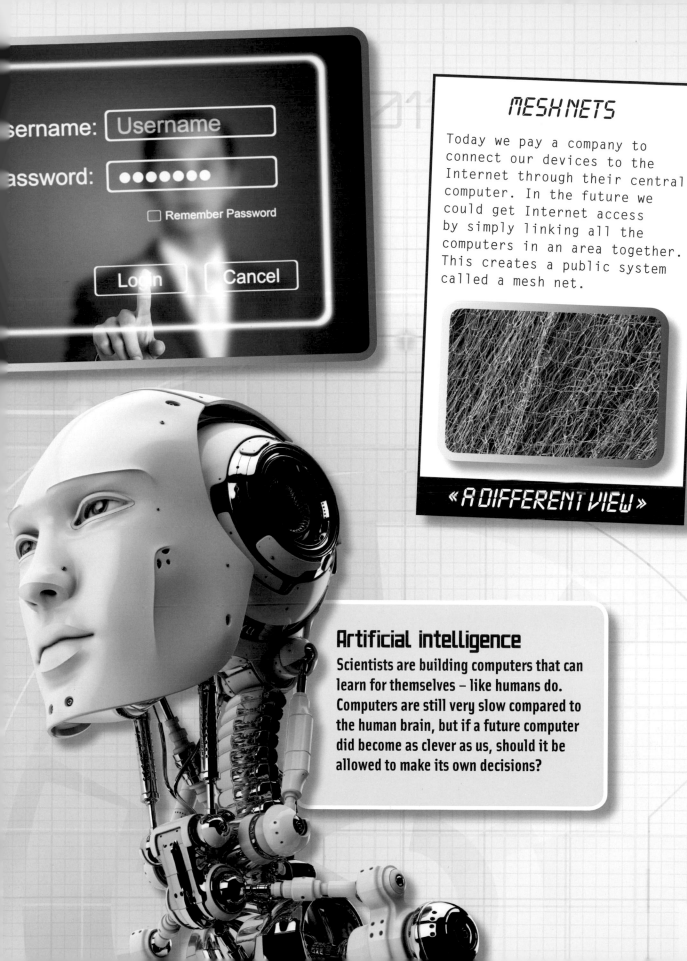

username: **Username**

password: ●●●●●●●

☐ Remember Password

Login   Cancel

Today we pay a company to connect our devices to the Internet through their central computer. In the future we could get Internet access by simply linking all the computers in an area together. This creates a public system called a mesh net.

« A DIFFERENT VIEW »

Artificial intelligence

Scientists are building computers that can learn for themselves – like humans do. Computers are still very slow compared to the human brain, but if a future computer did become as clever as us, should it be allowed to make its own decisions?

Glossary

app A small software application often loaded onto portable computers.

applications Software that allows a computer to be used for a particular purpose, such as a word processor.

circuit A collection of electrical components connected together.

data Items of information, normally organised as numbers.

diskettes A small floppy disk.

drive A device that reads files and saves files on a storage system, such as a CD, DVD, tape, or floppy disk.

electronic An electrical component that is able to switch on and off to control electrical current.

electrons Tiny particles that flow to create an electric current.

hacking To get access to a computer without permission.

hard disk A magnetic device inside a computer for storing files.

hardware The physical parts of digital technology.

Internet A network of computer networks that connects nine billion devices around the world.

mercury A liquid metal.

monitor A computer screen.

processor The part of a computer that runs programmes.

programmes A list of instructions followed by a computer.

programming language A series of terms used to write programmes.

search engine A system for finding items available on the web.

semiconductor A material that can both conduct and block electricity.

silicon The most common semiconducting material.

software The programmes that make a computer work.

virtual reality A three-dimensional world created by a computer.

web browser An application for looking at files on the Web.

Further Resources

Books

Ada Lovelace: The Computer Wizard of Victorian England (Who Was...?), Lucy Lethbridge. Short Books Ltd, 2004.

Let's Learn About Computers – Computer Software, Anneline Kinnear. Origin Books, 2013.

Computer, Mike Goldsmith and Tom Jackson, Dorling Kindersley, 2011.

Scratch Programming in Easy Steps, Sean McManus. In Easy Steps, 2014.

Raspberry Pi for Kids, Dennis Publishing, 2013.

The Computer (Tales of Invention), Chris Oxlade. Heinemann Library, 2011.

What's Next for Communication? (Future Science Now), Tom Jackson. Wayland, 2013.

Websites

http://windows.microsoft.com/en-GB/windows/history
The history of Microscoft and the Windows operating system.

http://scratch.mit.edu
Try out being a computer programmer with this language designed by MIT for beginners (Massachusetts Institute of Technology).

http://www.computerhistory.org/revolution
Timelines from the Computer History Museum in California.

http://computer.howstuffworks.com/pc.htm
The basics of personal computers from HowStuffWorks.

http://www.sciencemuseum.org.uk visitmuseum_OLD/galleries/computing.aspx
The computing section of London's Science Museum.

http://www.apple.com/uk/30-years
Check out this history of the Apple Macintosh computer.

Index